GU00950088

Weather Report

poems by

Rhonda Batchelor

Porcepic Books
an imprint of

Beach Holme Publishing
Vancouver

This book is published by Beach Holme Publishing, #226—2040 West 12th Ave., Vancouver, BC, V6J 2G2. This is a Porcepic Book.

We acknowledge the financial support of the Canada Council for the Arts, the Government of Canada through the Book Publishing Industry Development Program (BPIDP) and the assistance of the Province of British Columbia through the British Columbia Arts Council for our publishing activities and program.

The Canada Council for the Arts | Le Conseil des Arts du Canada

Editor: Joy Gugeler
Production and Design: Jen Hamilton
Cover Photographs: Charles Lillard
Author Photograph: Sandy Mayzell

Canadian Cataloguing in Publication Data

Batchelor, Rhonda, 1953-
  Weather report

  Poems.
  ISBN 0-88878-408-2

  I. Title.
PS8552.A825W42 2000   C811'.54   C00-910082-2
PR9199.3.B37572W42 2000

For you, Charles

". . .where a man arrives as far as he can,
not as far as he wishes."

Contents

Acknowledgements

Earlier versions of some of these poems first appeared in *ARC, Convolvulus, The Malahat Review, Poetry Canada Review* and *Prism international*. My thanks to the editors. A selection was also published in the chapbook *Waiting Game* (Reference West, Victoria, 1998). A Project Assistance Grant from the British Columbia Arts Council in 1997 was very much appreciated.

For their help (literary and otherwise), I am grateful to many friends: Patricia Young, Linda Rogers, Anne Kelly, Kerry Slavens, Margaret Blackwood, Liza (E.) Harris, Cathryn Dimock, Ian Callan and the late Robin and Sylvia Skelton. Georgina Montgomery, Bryony Wynne Boutilier, Jenny Winstone, Monica Turner and Sharon Churchill are still The Girls. I thank The Hawthorne Society, especially Sandy Mayzell, John Gould and Horst Martin, for carrying the torch when we lost three of our founding members. Joy Gugeler, editor of editors, I thank for her patience, professionalism and her profound insight. Michael Doyle, with his Irish generosity, made available his beautiful home on Pender Island when I most needed sanctuary. So, too, did David and Andrea Spalding, Kathleen Lightman and Terry Chantler, Georgina M. and Lawrence Pitt. Blessings on your Pender homes. Bruce Morgan of Virtual Consultants is my virtual angel and Alex Lavdovsky of Classic Engraving my artistic avenger.

Finally, and forever, my love to Ben and Joanna Lillard. Your dad would be proud.

Note: All quotes from Remy de Gourmont are from *Letters to the Amazon*, an inspiring but sadly out-of-print book published by Chatto and Windus (London) in 1931. This translation is by Richard Aldington. The music of George Ivan (Van) Morrison continues to give my life a soundtrack with soul.

Did ye get healed?
Yes.

Waterford Vase

It captured Sunday night's sunset.
Held Monday's sun.
It caught Tuesday night's firelight.
Look. It saved you some.

Vague Happiness

We begin to long for vague happiness which at the same time would be profound, close at hand and far off, soft and sharp, complicated delusive pleasures which are frightening or laughable from their folly. This desire knows only too well that no one has the power to heal its restlessness.

—Remy de Gourmont, *Letters to the Amazon*

Here to Feed Grace

who greets my arrival at the gate,
moves among my feet, along
the path wetly paved with
half-frozen December leaves,
leans on the door.

I fumble for the key,
carry my overnight bag
inside, take off my boots,
hang up my coat.

I am the season's warmth,
human kindness, giving
to be given
in return. There is a cry
to be let out
when Grace
has had her fill.

Under the Overhang

of the front porch, forced iris and tender *primula veris* bloom in clay pots, leaves serene. Beyond, everything is buried in winter, an unwelcome guest settling in. Oh, the kindness of friends who leave keys under stone angels. Ground level and snow-lit, this suite is full of books and straw hats. I try on a shiny blue boot but its owner's foot is dainty and I'm an outsized Alice.

When it's time to go home I'll have to walk
in the footprints of others, haltingly,
in unsuitable shoes, facing immutable spring.

Dunblane

March came in like a madman.
Patches of darker grey when we believed
the pewter sky was solid, of a piece,
and our private heartache
would save us.

Stars we gazed upon that cold night
a reminder how fleeting
small lives. In the vast
classroom of the universe,
we're forced to kneel
and tremble, the sky
not finished with us.

May's End

The robin's swan song,
insistent, urgently cheerful,
draws me to the window
where I see nothing more
than the sky finally clearing
in the west now that the sun has set.

Wet cedars droop into night.
I move through rooms
extinguishing lights,
when the bird's startled cry
calls me again.

The flat plane struggles to reveal
what's left of the longer view.
Not wanting reflection to confirm
how tired, how old, I look
beyond the pale moon of my face.
There is grace in the world's turning,
if not in the way I draw
the curtain, or turn to leave the room.

Full

Hunan
ginger beef
and salty smoked duck. My empty plate
a shiny disc.
Outside,
a strange glow over the neighbourhood
skyline with its white
observatory dome.

Look at this

My friends press close against the table's
bounty as the luminous platter
of the moon slides onto a velvet backdrop.
Familiar faces are
suddenly cast in light
radiant
as porcelain.

Gabriola

for Monica

She asks which aspect of the view I like best,
the pines on the foreshore, the point
of rock across the bay, or the
mountains, rain-hidden all day.
She asks this at night when all is dark.

Waves assault the sandstone beach,
wind boxes the trees.
Glass doors retain this lamp-lit room
and two friends at peace.
The rest of the world
beyond me.

Parameters of Grace

I went east and south but never greenward,
I went in and out but there was no road homeward.
—Gwendolyn MacEwen,
"Reviresco: In Memory of Padraig O'Broin"

Gwen, I wish you'd visit me even though it's Thursday and Thursdays you reserved for going mad. I've been reading the entrails of *Magic Animals*. I always thought you told your story well, if too briefly. If you'd drop by I'd break open the scotch I've been hoarding, get a fire going, bring two chairs to the window. Small white ferries will pass with their loads of mortal men. Island to island. We'll talk about those who drive us to the limits of love and compare our shades of loneliness. Tell me again about the parameters of grace. Or let's be silent and consider how words have let us down.

Aerial

She brings red wine and a photograph album
of aerial views taken from
a two-seater,
Desolation Sound
down to Oregon, snowy
mountains, blue-green coves.
It makes me want to distance myself
even more than I do by coming here
to stay in a house built high on a hill
with a view to die for. And later,
when she's gone off to navigate the
Celtic knot of roads from Galleon to Gunwhale,
I stay up
in the darkness imagining a cluster of lights
in the distance as a place to land. Black water
between me and a place with no pain.

Blooms Eternal

We'd gone ahead in the
stupid hope spring brings.

Now, spent by summer's
searing heat,
worn-out snapdragons
look ashamed at the
mess around them. The rest
never did
measure up. It was all
wrong; choice of plants,
places for them,
the poor soil,
lack of sun.

And it's too late to start over
(though leggy delphiniums are
on sale), too hot to bother.
Black aphids have won.
We sit with a catalogue
of latin names and a view
of the last geranium.

Backbone of the Moon

for Raymond Carver

Within the whiteness of its globe,
glowing whiter still, curled inward
like the spine of a child
in the womb,
the graceful arc,
an x-ray view
of the backbone of the moon.

When I described this to friends
they said
what a beautiful thing,
and that much I thought
I knew.

But this hot afternoon,
the summer solstice and
A New Path to the Waterfall,
a cat cuts through the shade of orange
day lilies, white
gulls steady over us. My wine glass
half full and not
what I'd thought. From this
comes a kind and generous answer.

Eclipse

The earth rolled over.
Between the sun and moon
our shadow fell.

On the next hilltop
people gathered,
upright silhouettes.

The lunar show was lengthy
so we turned
our binoculars on the sunset.
Fire engines flashed
along the waterfront.

Saturn appeared; a boy
on a wire fence swore
his naked eyes
could see its rings.
We could barely make
our way back down
the rocky trail. It was
dark and all

the familiar contours
fallen away.
Dogs ran about barking, rolling over
on the back of the still-warm earth.

Flight Paths

From my borrowed bit of paradise, the flight paths
of dragonflies, bright aqua, and the sky,
this most excellent canopy,
a route for
gulls and crows to chase
down through a corridor
of trees toward a distance
of blue sea with black islands
dilating at sunset.

Our daughter's eyes. Our son's.
Eyes that mirror my own and love,
they are still your finest gifts to me.

Mercurial

The artist phones in sick,
a mumbled message.
It's too hot,
gone haywire, degrees
of lies. It's insanity
to go outside,
to work
in such mutant weather.

The muggy night's left him weak; yesterday
was excess with nothing to show.
His studio is slow to release
last night's stale gathering. The west
window's thin curtain limp
against the feverish day.
A fly dies loudly
between the panes of glass.

Hours pass as the artist studies
an unfinished canvas.
The afternoon melts
from jazz to blues.
On the table a letter
so long composing
it no longer
has a destination.
Behind his eyes
red-veined patterns pulse,
negative, familiar.

As the dark
bleeds in he turns on
the lamp and reads

that Mercury is closest to the sun,
and to trace, while far-off sirens sound,
a thin red line, its progress as it
creeps along.

Unemployed Poet

You try on titles expecting
to summon the rest later.
You know you can do it; you're quick
to catch on. You wander around

and around
with a résumé in stanzas with
perfect line breaks,
no spelling mistakes,
vast experience and a date
of birth that may be
the only typo.

The city streets go by, your shoes
wear thin. You keep walking,
looking for a sign that says
Inquire Within.

Fight

It does not come from harm or hate
but from the rages and the guilt
that love necessitates.
—Dorothy Livesay, "The Quarrel"

You storm down the basement stairs
to get away from me. Turn
on the landing to hurl one more curse:
Woman!

My anger churns, a furious bile
of sarcasm and scorn.
There will be no apologies tonight,
every door slammed between us.

You fall asleep so easily,
your snores gall me as I write this.
Not an apology;
that will come
in the hesitant morning and go
without saying.

Weather Report

(on reading Eavan Boland's In a Time of Violence)

When the music stops, the spin cycle
has wrung the last drop and the words
I've been savouring echo,
I know the ache of being
a woman in middle age hungry for
a poem to grow old by.
                         Clouds gather over
the west, where all weather begins.
Our children
went out this morning,
their freckled skin covered with lotion.
Yet you and I assume
a mythological time when people
went about their lives, cheerful and
hatless under the sun.

I welcome clouds now, want
to mask the malignant brightness.
By lamplight it's safe
to write the memory of fresh-blown
linen, a simple warmth, to pray
this passion will be reborn
under our children's clear skin
when they read our voices
and hear a distant thunder.

Old Cat in Spring Sun

One more summer's all we can ask. One
short season of long days and
dry, starry nights. A sofa,
broad and broken-in, fading.
The dish kept full and waiting. Cool
water in a tin bowl.

Outside the window small birds
are bold. Ignore them. Sleep
a peaceful sleep.
Last incarnation
before paradise. The door
is open into the garden;
all creatures
may come and go.

out all morning with the cosmos. Sweating as I tear the creep of vetch from lemon marigolds. A headache blazes in the midsummer sky. I work until my knees wear through, until my gloveless fingers bleed. I don't stop for water from the coiled snake of garden hose or rest in the shade behind the shed. This is work. This is trying again to make sense of the days of catshit on the breeze, an infestation of aphids, of blackberry thorns.

I was up all night with you who can't get enough. Stars looked on and the bed overrun with California poppies. I atoned for their brazen beauty. Piled them on the path and swept them up before the shadows grew too long.

Tonight, after dinner, looks will be exchanged over the heads of children. Before our bed is turned, we will bathe and repair, to ask each other questions. Answers lost in exhausted sleep, before the baby wakes, before the moon sets.

Leash

It should be Thursday in this wind,
in my black felt hat, its brim
spotted by rain
just beginning.

People are shopping early for Christmas.
Many are driving cars on streets I can see
from here on the hill, a leather leash
around my hand. One eye on the dog,

but mostly I watch the city. Somewhere
a child squirms in a dentist's chair.
Someone looks at her watch.
On a quiet cul de sac
perhaps two women meet, two hours
before school lets out.

In that time I will have returned
with the dog and the leash. Would have hung
my coat and sodden hat, trying not to
think about the day,
the weather, or any damned thing.

January Sestina

Once I find the key, the door opens
and the hearth cries out for fire.
More than anything I'm grateful to be inside,
yet move, first thing, to the window.
Winter sun, double-glazed, keeps the cold
at bay. Turn up the thermostat. I'm here to rest.

Forget the job, kids, husband and the rest.
The next four days are open.
I've come down with a cold
that wants to extinguish my fire.
Fever illuminates the window,
lighting up the words I keep inside.

After one day of looking out from the inside
it seems all I can do is rest
and that nothing exists beyond the window.
I can't do much more than open
another beer, listen to Van sing *Give me the fire*
and wonder at this new year beginning so cold.

I toss and turn beneath an eiderdown. With cold
feet, I'm lonely for my love to slip inside
my bed, to touch me at the source of the fire.
Only then can I sleep, only then rest
in the arms of the one who can open
me, release the words, break the window.

All my dreams fly out the window.
They dance away with the stars and are cold
mysteries while I'm left behind, inside.
It's just as well. I need this solid rest
when stars and ghosts steal my fire.

I bring wood from outside to feed the fire.
Rain replaces sun at the window.
I watch an eagle ascend and rest
in mid-flight. To heal my cold
I pause, too—inside.
Hibernation, eyes open.

This is all I can do. Just rest in this cold
month. Imagine a snow-covered greenhouse; inside
tender words are ready to open.

Solo

A day dark with rain. Reach
to the lamp to find it
already on.
How can it be this light
is not light enough?

Nothing shines bright or warms
but our children and this love for you.

Lift the shade.
Part the veil.
Nothing ceases
like the rain when
you lead me to the deep
warmth of your bed. Nothing

beyond the light of you,
your eyes, reflecting my fire,
making it two.

Conqueror

I still see your entrance into my solitude, my terror, and soon my joy at seeing one like you moving in me with the simplicity of a conqueror.

—Remy de Gourmont

I still believed in romance,
although no one asked for my hand
until you,
making up
for lost time,
looking at forty, simply reached
across the table. You
spoke it as a question, but I recall
a statement.
        Marry me.

Anticipation heightened
every day and night, those heady first months.
Yet, the day before our wedding I sat crying
on the rocks on Anderson Hill,
in the low September sun,
waiting for a sign

to come with the dark.

Impossible Desire

. . . impossible desire carves fidelity.
—Remy de Gourmont

No longer
what we imagined.

Forgetfulness sets in
and soothes the pain of a missing
limb. Roots push all the deeper.
I'm not going anywhere.

Climb into me.
My arms offer
high, spare shelter.
Feel the sureness of me
as impossible desire abates.
Pay no mind to the vanishing
shoreline.

Chanson

Sweet friend, I'm caught
in uncertainty, hardly daring
to look at you
in case my gaze reveals
my confusion.

If you don't want
to be transcended
this courtliness is wrong.

When you stand close
I tremble, afraid
you will notice, afraid
you won't. This fear
holds me abject and
too much alone.

Prescription

In his cramped, green examination room
the doctor says he's worried
about how I'm bearing up. Reminds me
not to forget my own needs. At the pharmacy,
waiting on pills, I make a list in my head of things
I need. A miracle.
Money. Someone to walk the dog, to shop,
cook, clean and help with homework.
Time, and silence.
To make love.

The pharmacist calls my married name,
sells me something to let me sleep.
I carry it home in a white bag and wonder
how many refills
before this is over.

Birthday

Remember the sun on the bed at St. Andrew's?
Your hair was still red, and it burned in the fiery
afternoons of sex.
I remember this

now as we lie together on my birthday, trying
a new, queen-size bed. Weak
February sun, children at school, telephone
off the hook.
Let's remember

it took years
of separation to bring us together
to this marriage bed.

Hold me now, love. Turn from the failings
of aging bodies, scars, surgery.
Rest with me, your skin against mine.
Whisper the old words,
recapture the sun.

Secret Garden

We meet in June. Drink wine and relax into big chairs as music plays. Dinner is made from whatever we find. Before dark we go outside to the secret garden, take in the cosmos and the moonflower that blooms below the bedroom window, the fragrant colours winding and climbing. More secret still, the names we breathe out over the morning, wet, like dew. Flowers unfolding in hidden places. The private view.

Glad Ghost

Think of beautiful women and do not desire them. Raise your heart
above their beauty, rejoice that they are glad with their lovers and, if
they lose breath on the way, charitably extend to them a spiritual hand.

—Remy de Gourmont

At the end of the evening when she's replete
with wine and wise words, she may
kiss his cheek as he helps her on with
her coat.
He'll ask again if she's
all right, offer his bed,
will sleep on the floor. He'll
wave goodbye, spiritual hand raised
in defeat.

She stops beneath a streetlight,
looks up. In the dark
an airplane drones.
She feels the weight of its heavy wings.

He'll dream he's drifting down
by parachute as she approaches
his house. She has the key
ready, runs the last few steps.
He'll concentrate
as he tries again
to wave.

Fifth Night

He can stand his own company just so long;
it doesn't bear the scrutiny of hours this close.
There's a danger when he has this much time;
the focus grows too sentimental and soft
or else turns harsh in its blaming, cuts too sharp.
Either way, it's likely too late to completely heal

the wounds made or to forgive and heal
the hurt they've carried far too long.
Nothing hurts as much as sharp
scorn from one so close.
It doesn't take much to level her aim to the soft
belly of his fear, take her time

to lash out in passing, or allow all time
to carry an unspoken barb. How can he heal
from a future blow? His heart goes soft
with imagined pain. He's waited this long
fearing the worst to justify seldom coming close.
Yet picture their lives apart, how sharp

a shock that would be. A sharp
division of past and no-future time.
There would be no wound left to close.
Other lives than his left to heal.
There are papers to sign and in the long
and short of it there's no time to be soft.

He sits with his thoughts as soft
firelight tempers the dark. At 12:20 sharp
tomorrow she'll board the ferry for the long
journey, hoping this time
he'll have settled something, begun to heal.
He'll know when he holds her close.

Outside, a cold December moon seems close
enough to touch. He wants it to shine in a soft
halo while she sleeps and heal
all traces of the scars whose sharp
edges he's memorized for all time.
Like drinking to forget, it's not long

before he's willing to believe in the sharp
swimmer who will make it to the estuary this time.
He can stand his own company just so long.

Ciphers

The only sounds, my laboured breath
and the old rake as it scrapes the wet earth.
It will freeze tonight.
In the dusk one star readies itself as
geographies form
at the roadside. This nation seems one
vast backyard to be
tidied before first snow. In Montreal,
Kingston, Saskatoon, others burn
leaves of poplar or maple, with smoke rising
into a harsher winter than mine.
When it's time
to go in, make a pot of tea,
they'll put rakes aside and stand a moment
in the cold, their breath making
wordless poems that float there
like ciphers.

Storm

for Robin

The old year locks us in.
Whisky's low. One child
with the flu; the other doesn't know
what to do with herself
but won't walk the dog
or return the videos.
Tired of TV, you read
magazines or sleep
in your chair, head
bowed to your chest.
Awake, you complain of the cold,
your aching leg, that you can't work.
Snap at the kids, at me.

In my room my white
desk reflects the snowlight of
weird sculpture forming outside.
The cedar tree is a totem, a solemn
albino bird.

At dusk I plow
a furrow to the corner store.
A pair of eagles grip a high branch in
swirling snow. Their nest has fallen, yet
side by side, proud heads crowned, white,
they wait.

Pilgrim

From a faraway place
with a noble tradition
a high wind blows
cirrus clouds
to pale fragments
in a blue eye
porous and cool.
From a sleepless place
peopled by strangers,
where loved ones come
and go.
My beloved
dances in firelight,
sparks shuddering
into a chilly sky.

Shadow Weather

Things are looking up.
Some of the old energy,
sapped by radiation, back in your step;
your latest book
garners a recognition that surprises you.

Christmas comes and goes, the snowstorm
of the century. You make it as far as the path's end
to photograph our neighbour's buried '64 Chrysler.

In the new year you feel so good
you tell the doctor at the cancer clinic to spare you
news that would spoil your day. A friend
is waiting to take you to lunch. It feels like spring
the way Victoria can in January.
The doctor takes you at your word.
You call me to say you've been given
a clean bill of health.
I can hardly believe it.

In February you sleep more, but badly, and with pills.
Entries in your day-book dwindle. Plans
and projects, poems and phone calls on hold.
One morning in March you stay in bed, say you've got
that flu going around. After two weeks I tell the doctor
you're not eating, losing weight.
He looks at me with pity.

What I don't know is how much
you know, or if you honestly believe health
will be restored. You seem so surprised.
Do I make your death real by bringing in
the hospice nurses? At the end
there is no time to ask, or tell.
When you call to me, just as the
small hours close over, there is only time
for the briefest farewell.

Can you hear me? I ask, and you,
with your last breath,
take away all the answers.

Visible Contents

A Double Phantasy

Hush! I said to myself. I will sleep, and the ghost of my silence can go forth, in the subtle body of desire, to meet that which is coming to meet it. Let my ghost go forth and let me not interfere. There are many intangible meetings, and unknown fulfillments of desire.

—D. H. Lawrence, "Glad Ghosts"

There's a dream where the contents are visible,
Where the poetic champions compose.
Will you breathe not a word of this secrecy?
Will you still be my special rose?
—Van Morrison, "Queen of the Slipstream"

Inseparable

I've imagined so many things I imagine I've imagined you. Through pure desire or sheer will, or simple magic, I've given you form and touch, speech and action.
But now it seems you are able to take yourself away.

You are no less of a man for being imagined. You are the sum and selected parts of many, a myth perpetuated by my own conviction. A phantasy, clinging thistle-like to the fabric of days and nights.

In my mind, though apparently not in yours, we are inseparable.

Manifest

When I have courage enough to think about it, I suppose I must be dead. Nothing short of death explains it. I have become a spirit whose destiny belongs to this woman of flesh and blood.

She is beautiful. Mine isn't a destiny without pleasure. Our lovemaking, the very heat of our joined bodies, is manifest.

Equinox

Flames lick the log, send fireworks up the flue. Admire the yellow thrust of daffodils, the deep crimson throats of tulips open on the table. Ice melts in the hold of my tongue. Footsteps, a knock.

You hold out cherry blossom torn from my own tree and lilac from someone else's. Wet shoes, cold hands, rain on your face.

We move to the fire casting glances amber whisky drinks in. The ice melts but dilutes nothing.

Tryst

When the light is dim, the wine cold,
let me know how good...

When the bedroom door is locked
against the disapproving world,

describe the one we can't
touch, or name.

In your embrace I move.
Intimate pleasure, a secret shared.

Our fingers meeting
in colourless hair.

Eyes That Mirrored Mine

I remember the first time you appeared. It was early summer, early evening with the first stars. The sunset still aglow. I sat in the car, facing the Olympian mountains that caught the light and offered it back, transformed.

A woman stopped to take a photograph, then turned her camera, half in jest, toward her beloved. He stood still, relaxed and happy from a day in the sun, smiling at the moon rising behind her, horned and slim. I watched them continue their walk, arm in arm, into the last of the sunset.

When I turned my gaze, finally, to the east again, there you were. At first only a dark form, then closer into focus. Your head was down, eyes fixed on the ground, your hands deep in pockets. I had to get out of my car and step into your path or you might have walked right past. I half expected an apparition, but when I put out my hand you were solid, warm. Your blue eyes met mine. You needed a shave.

Spirits

My own can be lifted with alcohol, another earthly pleasure. It always seems at hand when I'm with her. Once or twice I've felt the slim weight of a pint of whisky in the inner pocket of my jacket, yet can't recall having been anywhere to purchase it. More often she has wine, white and cold. Long after my initial high has turned restless, she continues to drink. The wine emboldens her.

If I'm still with her by morning, I'll bring her a cold cloth for an aching head. Such mornings, adding milk to her coffee, I pity her more than myself.

Never Mind the Weather

While I drove, you sat darkly beside me, pounding tape after tape into the player, rejecting them in turn. I broke the ultimate silence with a comment on the beauty of the night sky. *Never mind the weather*, you snapped. *Let me take you to bed.*

Mysticus

We were naked. We were sipping hot Irish from clay mugs, lounging by a fire. I enjoyed a slow, mounting warmth and stroked her thigh as she read aloud from a book of dreams. This is a dream, I thought, and felt the hair rise on the back of my neck. She was reading about a succubus, a demon who assumes female form to consume men in their sleep. She turned to look at me then, strangely, with half-closed eyes.

Covering the Waterfront

Sometimes, travelling from one locale to another, I had to make do with a mute and shadowy companion until we reached our destination. A certain beach just outside of town. A riverside motel I'm fond of. A cabin up-coast.
Was that it? Could I divine you only near water? I've been back to the waterfront several times at sunset.

Here's where we walked in the spring, on the wharf where wind rocks the boats. *Elusive Destiny. The Siren,* with her twin-tailed fish/woman duality half-hidden by black water. *Pacific Gale* sits low, ready to ride out any weather. *Amazing Grace* opposite the sign announcing Seaplane Tours.

To just board a plane, fly somewhere. In the sky, a jet stream bisects my wish. Another sign. *Persons using this wharf do so at their own risk.*

Sleeping

Her sleep must be solid for it includes me, fixes somehow. Tonight we are in a motel set back from the highway, under tall trees, close enough to the river to hear its murmur. In a tangle of sheets, I study her; breasts I have stroked and kissed, long legs that have wrapped around me. She takes my breath away. Gives it back.

Not Sleeping

Solitude is crowded.
Last night everyone swept through this place,
their chatter constant.
Later, the tall trees outside the window ran rings
around my sleep.
Stars through the skylight seemed more distant.
By dawn the voices quieted to yours and mine.

A Still Part of the Stream

The first thing I can recall this time is staring down a heron. The great bird stood motionless on a peninsula of stones protecting a still part of the stream. I became aware of the warmth of the sun on my head. Reluctantly I turned toward the sound of distant traffic. The yellow leaves on the trees signalled fall. I couldn't remember anything of summer.

I saw her then, sunning herself on the grassy slope. A few, scattered cottages nearby. She lay on her stomach with a paperback. Her lips moved as though in silent prayer. I moved a step closer. She looked up, smiling, eyes squinting in the low, autumn sunlight.

Small Consolation

I could press a button and hear your voice. Small consolation.
It's a poor tape, mostly engine noise,
the recorder and microphone hidden in the back seat,
switched on for our drive along the coast, kept on for miles.

Your left hand resting on my thigh and I am, for the time, content.
I ask if I should roll up my window. This bit of silence
your shrug of indifference.

It's bright midday when I say, to be funny,
In this fog, so late at night, how can I avoid you?

You can't, you say,
You will crash right through me.

No Whisky

If it wasn't so dark, wasn't raining so damned hard, I'd take a walk.
I've been waiting since sundown. I've made a fire.
Made three pots of tea and let them grow cold. There's no whisky.

You must come through the rain.
You must find me.

Signifying Nothing

A storm was raging, all noise and fury. I was by the sea. Except for a Siamese following me from room to room I was alone, but seeking you. I called your name, softly, urgently. But not your name, only *Love, Love,* over and over, through barren rooms, the cat at my heels.

I climbed stairs to the attic, found you crouched on a mattress, frightened of the storm, or of me. I approached slowly.

You lay passively while I tried to arouse you. You kept your eyes tightly shut.

Lilac

I was in a hospital room with a female visitor who held a large, black photograph album, spilling over with pictures of my life. My house, my friends, my children, cats, even my car. I couldn't deny that the woman beside me was the bride in the wedding photos; the smiling groom and the proud father the man in my mirror.

She turned the pages and spoke slowly, carefully, as to a child.
"And here she is again, in the backyard with one of the kittens."
I looked, instead, at the lilacs in the background and could recall breaking off a bouquet.

I'm still here, waiting in this rain-soaked wood.
No longer sure who it is I'm waiting for.

Old-Fashioned Typewriter

A small, oval-shaped likeness of you in the bottom corner
of a plastic identification card, folded papers and a photograph of
a young girl I know to be your daughter. Poised blond head
wearing your expression:
resignation or chagrin.

The photo and papers have fallen from a metal-cornered, black
leather carrying case resembling an early box camera but
containing an old-fashioned typewriter. It's early morning and
I'm in a kitchen I know is yours. The photo, the box, the typewriter,
on a counter in front of me. I don't know where you are.

Outgoing Message

Have to leave here soon. Clear everything as though I won't be back. Wash the plate and cup and put them away. Hang the dishcloth. It's raining and I forgot the umbrella, its handle carved like a duck's head. Plump the pillows, smooth the quilt.

Pack up the few books, the tiresome tapes. Close all the blinds, empty the cold tea from the pot. If a house wants you to go, you have to go.

Something changed overnight. The ovulation of the moon, clouds moving in. As soon as the rain lets up, write a short note to leave by the phone, an apology for erasing the outgoing message.

Black Ice

You approach a red brick house in winter snow. As the door is opened by an unseen hand, you lose your footing on the icy path. I am watching this from afar. You move in slow motion, as one moves through water. I'm frozen as you begin to fall toward me, then right yourself, regain your balance and continue on the path. I can't see the face of the one who lets you in.

After

Maybe today. Yes. I'm almost sure of it. The atmosphere is right. So much rain. The eaves of my house overflow and a heavy stream pours down the front porch, quick footsteps. More than once I've gone to check. Otherwise, it's quiet. Only the rain and the company of the fire I've made.

Here, you can dry your wet clothes. Let me towel your hair, lean to kiss you. Yes, like that. So good. To see you again. Hold you. No arguments, no questions, no drinking. Yes, my cheeks are flushed, but it's so warm in here. Hold me. Help me to undress. How I love your smile.

Almost asleep and the fire's in need of fuel. The rain, now driven by wind, batters the window. *Listen*, I say. And you, in a far-off voice, say *Do you hear footsteps?* I go to look and when I turn back you're gone. Again.

Still Breathing

One can't go on writing forever about how hard it is to breathe.
—Václav Havel

*Love is physical, all love has a physical basis, because the physical
alone exists and the soul is an invention of the Sorbonne....*
—Remy de Gourmont, *Letters to the Amazon*

State of the Union

There is no union
but a vanishing point
growing smaller
as I fall behind
in the flat land of the
still breathing.

In the bath I open
my eyes, see my body,
breasts, belly, knees.
I could be an archipelago
in a foamy sea,
or anything but this.

It's Late

too late, and I'm tired,
                a bit drunk,
so damned
                empty.
This grief demands
                pain
so pure, so entire
I can't
give
any more.

In bed I imagine
your touch,
your soft cries of love.

                Oh love
these are my cries.
Not soft.

Impossible

Wanting to be
alone,
to be
not alone.
My soul
and body
at war.

Longing
for the kiss
impossible.

Before,
when you'd touch
your lips to the back
of my neck,
I'd shiver and
wipe it away.
I can't imagine
(n)ever doing that again.

Deep in the Mirror

I'd like to keep you where you used to put
Yourself: deep in the mirror, far away
From everything.
—Rainer Maria Rilke, *Requiem for a Woman*

This isn't about the mirror,
but the soul in exile there.
The soul of the body
that fed upon itself.

Before you entered in you said
you had expected this deceit
having been so healthy,
so long.

I blamed the strong tea you drank
as you worked before dawn,
years of cigarettes, before Ben was born.

It's never going to go away,
your voice reported home,
and to me, awaiting word,
it was a lover's pledge.

Your soul entered in,
reluctant but resigned,
a place where words began to fail you.

Your last communiqué:
So tired.

The mirror
was a bride's gift to her groom.
I'm glad it carried you through.

Leave the Key

I think you'd be amused, secretly proud,
to know that two hours after your death
the children and I delivered
Ben's newspapers.

In the fresh light of that
lush Oak Bay morning, green
grass, spring blossoms, birdsong,
everything sweet, gentle,
unreal.

Up Central from Island, along Newport
with large houses set back from
wide, tree-lined avenues.

We barely spoke, each of us
struck dumb by the day.
My pockets full of tissues.
Jo and I took turns holding Sam's leash.

At Windsor Park, by the cricket green,
papers done, we let Sam run
with a poodle while I tried to
exchange small talk with her owner.

When we returned home we found
a white van in the drive.
Ben and Jo lingered in the basement,
choosing not to see you go.

But I watched from our front hallway,
suddenly so narrow
as the men turned the gurney,
and you left home,
head-first and forever.

Postscript

I leave the house, the phone,
the flowers, casseroles, sympathy cards.
The press calling for details.
He leaves a wife and two young children.

Between the swings and the tennis court
I examine the surfaces
of three wooden picnic tables.
When the kids were small the neighbourhood
fathers met here, summer evenings,
giving mothers a break after dinner.
The kids haywire and joyous until dark.
The men turned a blind eye
to clothing soaked by sprinklers,
to big kids with water guns,
swapped gossip
and bad jokes instead, while they idly carved,
with Glenn's knife, or Terry's, their own
initials in the tabletop.
We were here,
in our prime, as fathers, as friends.

But the tables I study are new, uncarved,
and when two young nannies arrive with toddlers,
sandpails, juice boxes,
I turn away before my tears
upset the little ones.

Mirror After Mirror

For all my talk of mirrors, there's only one
in my bedroom. A modest
wood-framed rectangle
angled to reflect head and shoulders
and what's behind.

This isn't about the mirror,
but the photo of us below.
In our poet-black spring
jackets, your arms around me, fingers laced
protectively. My arms around you, too.
I'm wearing your grandma's
opal ring. I'd lost your other grandma's
diamonds, back when I was pregnant.

This isn't about the ring; there are other rings,
dark circles under our eyes—subtly shaded
by the elegance of black and white.
We're smiling,
yet the eyes have it.

What is it? Doubt? Fear?
Today I look closer.

Bride

The nightgown you loved
bodice cut low, satin ribbon tangled,
is wearing out, wearing thin.
In the dark with the
doors locked, I sit on the edge
of the bed. Bare feet against the floor
where your life left you.

I covered you with this blanket, then walked
slowly through the house, twice around
hallway, kitchen, living room,
pausing at this bedroom door like a
bride on her wedding night,
unprepared for what I needed to know.

The Rat

for Ted Hughes

Today in my yard, the grey rat,
stiff on a green bed of moss.
Bright fleck of blood
for the season.
Most of his tail gone.
I buried him
beneath a mound
of wet leaves from the cherry tree,
against the back hedge where the cats
can't get at him
anymore.

I've been laying down souls
like mulch. The odour
clings to me;
sweet decay, the odour
of earth.

Ghost Waving

In dreams you are
a gracious presence, a man come back
from a long journey. But last night
you kept appearing and
disappearing, a shadowy spirit
just behind the window.

Fog drifts around the house
as I pour my morning coffee.
I want to tell you I have plenty
of photographs; there's no need
to haunt me. It's cold comfort
if you've no other way
of coming home.

Strawberries

Allowing myself one, red, taste only.
Sacrifice
manifest in this succulent
gesture.
The scent of summer
when I close my eyes.
Breathe.

Where are you this afternoon?

Tragic

I want to call you, say
I'm alone.
Take the evening ferry.

Dinner on the deck
while the sun sets.
Pour your drink into mine.

So lonely I turn on the
television and there's Dietrich
kissing her own angel,
in black and white.

Lament

If I could go there now,
let myself in, lay myself down
on your pillows and look about
at those articles that shimmer
from being touched by you,
I would touch myself
in summoning you.
This might be wrong,
but necessary.

Widow

I'm driving home from work, a warm evening
in late spring. Hours of daylight left.
This is a year after your death. Two years.
Nothing and everything's the same.
I've put in my hours at the shop.
The regulars are fond of me and ask
how I'm doing, how the children are.
Fine, I say. *They're fine.*

I might turn down to the
waterfront to see how
the sea's doing. Sometimes
couples stroll hand in hand unaware
how hard I study them.

The first hour home is a blur
of checking in, phone messages, mail,
e-mail, the whereabouts of children,
sleep-over plans, what's for dinner, let me
just change my clothes, could someone
please feed these cats.

And then at some point, one point, I'm alone
with hours to fill. I could do
something, phone someone. I should do
laundry, Jo's baseball uniform needed
for tomorrow's game. I could walk somewhere.

First I'll have a glass of wine and listen
to the I-coulds and the I-shoulds argue
in circles around the silence. I'll play
some Van Morrison for hope and comfort.
I may decide I'm just tired.

When I finish the glass and look out
from my favourite window, the arguments
give up and go away.
It comes to this: it's dusk now and
I'm not going anywhere.

What You Left

Ten, maybe fifteen thousand books.
Lousy credit but no debts. Life insurance.
Walls dense with art. Four huge cabinets
crammed with paper: correspondence, clippings, articles, drafts, and
thirty years of journals.
A suspect collection of country and western tapes.
A radial-arm saw.
A few empty vodka bottles, one down inside your
overstuffed reading chair.
An eight-foot Swede saw.
A ten-speed bike and oversize helmet.
Three decades of plaid shirts and corduroy.
An entire drawer of handkerchiefs.

Your poems, histories, friends.
Your mother.
Ben and Jo.
Me.

Ephemera.

Good for You

If you knew, my dear friend, what they have done to my flat, where everything knew and loved you! These poor things are now incapable of knowledge, love, and any other feeling. They lie piled up in corners, wounded perhaps, with nothing left of the simple life bestowed upon them by daily use. I can think of nothing else and write of nothing else on this borrowed table where I am making uncertain loops with difficulty....

—Remy de Gourmont

The basement a metaphor.
Lonely hours, shifting and sorting.
Discovering fragments, past lives, relics
of your intelligence, fears and a larger-than-life
soul.
I cursed you, wanting
to leave it all in place, in peace,
but heard you whisper
Good for you, love,
the way you would.
No hard feelings. No point.
Just this getting on.

This Morning

The kids are still asleep. One of the kittens
leans from an open window to bleat at a crow.
Some of your files stacked on the table:
Fisheries, Bella Coola, Jones Creek circa 1979.
We were only lovers then.
I turn a sheet
of tea-stained paper in my hands.

> *Vision lives too close to*
> *my fingers,*
> *this morning*
> *you are not what I needed to say.*

Kissing the Ghosts Away

We both knew
who the ghosts were, named them
friends and familiars. Spirits
hiding in the basement, the whole house
whispering. I'd listen
on my knees at the vent, praying
I was wrong.

As for me, my ghostly companion
found a way into your dreams, too;
would leave me and drift down
through floorboards to settle
like a sleepwalker in your bed.
Even in our deepest
locking together,
even then, we were
never alone. All those years,
faces drifted overhead, mouths gaping.
I tried to kiss the ghosts away.
I never imagined
you'd join their ranks.
More and more ghosts
but no one to be haunted with.

Troubadour

The young man with a ladder
at my bedroom window promises
to mind my moonflower. I have
pointed it out and told him
to feel free to trample anything
else. It's glass
he's replacing, a pane
that's been cracked since another
man, on a different ladder,
brandished a paint-scraper with
too much force. But this
young man, lean and blond,
someone's son or sweetheart,
is self-conscious as I watch him climb.
When he begins to tap at the old
glass, he slips up; something gives.
Blood flows, drips,
from his hand, down
through the scented air and into
the thirsty ground.

It's the same ground in which
I bury a portion
of your ashes.
I dream you climb in at my window,
my troubadour,
to find me, *nightgown twisted,*
and the breasts you'd *never had enough of*
waiting for you.

I go on waiting. Dreams of you
elusive and fewer.
The moonflower
died this winter,
has not come back.

True Romancing

. . .*and the Lord walks on a summer night.*
—Van Morrison, "These Are the Days"

And here is a burning bush,
or so it seems, lit brilliantly

by low sun in early evening.
Mid-August,

blue and dried grasses.

I want someone
to rise over the crest of the highest

hill, to meet me.
A marine fog rolls in on a cool breeze.

Look at me. Waiting on an outcome, a miracle.
A saviour.

Blackberry

All summer I've watched
the blackberry vines
outside your study.
You used to love
their frenzied growth,
the branches clawing
at the window by your desk.

Yesterday I gathered the last
dark berries of September.
Overripe and mouldy, they fell
to the ground at my touch.
I came away with less
than half a pie and angry
scratches.
That's what happens
when you leave things.

Port of Angels

I read your poems
to your own lost one;
how you've walked and worn
an "egg-shaped circle" around
Ray's grave, keeping warm
as you talk to him.

Here, on this side, I have no grave
to visit; my husband's ashes circled
north to Alaskan waters, east
to an inland lake, south
to a great river. Some stayed here
in the west, in Victoria, where
he'd finally found home,
and named it such,
before he left us.

All my pacing takes place in my head,
and not so much a circle
as back and forth,
to and fro, and
either way,

I don't get very far
from a central truth.

You look north
while I look south, over
the same turbulent waters, under
a changeable coastal sky,
trying to keep warm,
talking to the wind.

Blue Leaving

for Ben Batchelor (1914–1999)

A '65 Ford Comet, powder blue,
my first car when I lived at home,
a gift from my father who said *It's your turn*
to run errands and play chauffeur. Dreams
of escape were narrowed. I had to field
the chores and follow a mapped-out road.

A summer job, teaching art, had me on the road
from park to park, saying *For sky, use blue,*
and make the barn smaller at the top of the field.
At four o'clock, lessons done, I'd head home
hot and longing for the kind of dreams
I'd hear on the AM radio when I'd turn

it up loud—before I'd have to turn
back into the dutiful one on the right road.
I helped with dishes, watched TV, my dreams
on hold until the streetlights shone blue
into my room. Across town my boyfriend was at home
in a house of his own. The Strawberry Fields

of Lennon, in my mind, were the fields
behind my lover's house and at night I'd turn
on psychedelic highways far from home,
wild and reckless, the road
twisted into morning. His blue
eyes haunting me long after the dream.

At seventeen I moved on from mere dreams,
looked at larger maps and widened the field
of my territory. I'd had enough of feeling blue.
I had to climb in and finally turn
the wheel down a wide, new road
that would take me far from home.

There's still a place for me at home
and sometimes I go there in dreams.
After years on this road
I want to stop by a green field.
And even if I could, I would never turn
or go back through those years. Blue

eyes are my children's eyes. A field
runs to each horizon. When it's their turn
I will wish them comets, morning blue.

Sitting Alone

in a small restaurant. Early dinner as shopkeepers close up, flip
the signs in the windows, turn the keys and hurry off.

Rain, threatening all day, begins in a fine mist.
Candles on the tables. Music on the radio rolls over

like the random sound of car tires on wet road. I am
the only customer and the waiter is bored. I object

to hollandaise on the broccoli,
he brings another glass of white.

I tell him it's my birthday. He serves me
complimentary cake and I ask him to join me, offer a fork.

There's a lie in here somewhere, hidden like a shiny coin
in the devil's food. I'm half hoping he'll find it.

Watcher

It's a lie—I'm not tired of you,
I'm tired of myself.
I just want to be able to see you,
watch you fall in love with someone else
and never notice me.
—Cecilia Vicuna, "Beloved Friend"

He would be a watcher,
a shadow in a corner
of your room,
                    waiting
for you to come
home in the evening.
If there is
a faint trace of
                    sadness
put it down
to the widow below,
her boiled dinner,
her radio.
Your own heart is light
as you spread the cloth
over the low table,
                    unwrap
the cheese, open the *vin rouge*
to breathe.

When you have bathed, arranged your hair
and kissed the image in your mirror,
                  there's a knock at the door.
His heart's beat
is yours. You're held
and he's held.

He could no sooner leave
than not love you,
would sooner watch you,
                  in love,
invisible,
than close his eyes
and never see you
at all.

Healing Game

. . . and you live right here in the day
till we get the healing done.
—Van Morrison,
"Till We Get the Healing Done"

I linger in the yard, idly throwing pinecones
for a small spaniel to chase and chew and not retrieve.
Overnight a storm blew in, obscuring first the moon
and now the sun. Early spring is a muddy palette
of greens and browns. The only promise of warmth
hides in the muted red of an arbutus trunk—and that
proves cold enough. But as my hand caresses
its seamless curve, the broad smoothness recalls
a lover's naked back.

Soon I'll chop some wood, make lunch, then sit
watching wind churn the surface of the sea.
I've no clue if you're with me, or in
those rainclouds over Vancouver Island, or the spirit
of that eagle soaring just off the point.
The point is—and it's clearer each day
I'm without you—you will not be forgotten.
But neither, love, will my own life,
neither will my joy.

Remember

You drove me downtown just before dawn
in Vicki's '64 Chrysler to meet the bus
bound for the first ferry to Pender.
It was January '97. There was no money
and much to fear. I was getting away.
You took me as far as you could.

I rode the Pat Bay #70 along
the rural roads of Saanich, thinking
you should be with me to see the sun
rising up an orange ball over the
frosted fields. It was a sun that said
Remember me like this.

In my mind I placed you in the seat beside me
and we were quiet as the bus engine droned.
I wanted to say how this was Lane and Crozier territory
we were passing through, how they'd claimed it,
turned Saanichton into Saskatchewan,
or *vice versa*, just by living here awhile.
That our cruising along together was right
and *like* them somehow. Two poets married
to this strange journey.

As I recall it now
you *did* take me all the way.
I'll always remember
"Love Me Do" on the car radio.
Your sweet kiss
before you pulled away.

Rhonda Batchelor is the author of two collections of poetry, *Bearings* and *Interpreting Silence*. She has been anthologized in *Windhorse Reader: Choice Poems of 1994*, *Because You Loved Being a Stranger: 55 Poems Celebrate Patrick Lane*, and *New Life in Dark Seas: Brick Books 25*. She lives in Victoria, BC, and is the manager of The Hawthorne Bookshop. She is also the publisher of Reference West chapbooks.